The California Missions

by Ann Heinrichs

Content Adviser: Marlene A. Smith-Baranzini,
Associate Editor,
California Historical Society

Social Studies Adviser: Professor Sherry L. Field,
Department of Curriculum and Instruction, College of Education,
The University of Texas at Austin

Reading Adviser: Dr. Linda D. Labbo,
Department of Reading Education, College of Education,
The University of Georgia

COMPASS POINT BOOKS

Minneapolis, Minnesota

Compass Point Books
3722 West 50th Street, #115
Minneapolis, MN 55410

Visit Compass Point Books on the Internet at *www.compasspointbooks.com* or e-mail your request to *custserv@compasspointbooks.com*

Photographs ©: Hulton Getty/Archive Photos, cover, 11, 14, 36; North Wind Picture Archives, 5, 10, 13, 17, 24, 26, 27, 35; PhotoDisc, 6; Stock Montage, 7, 37; Joel W. Rogers/Corbis, 9; Archivo Iconografico, S.A./Corbis, 12; Scala/Art Resource, NY, 15; Mark E. Gibson/Visuals Unlimited, 19; Eda Rogers, 20, 21, 22, 23, 29, 38; California Historical Society, North Baker Research Library, Templeton Crocker Collection, FN-25092, 25; Museo Naval, Madrid, 31; Charles and Josette Lenars/Corbis, 33; John D. Cunningham/Visuals Unlimited, 40.

Editors: E. Russell Primm, Emily J. Dolbear, and Deborah Cannarella
Photo Researchers: Svetlana Zhurkina and Jo Miller
Photo Selector: Linda S. Koutris
Designer: Bradfordesign, Inc.

Library of Congress Cataloging-in-Publication Data
Heinrichs, Ann.
 The California missions / by Ann Heinrichs.
  p. cm. — (We the people)
 Includes bibliographical references and index.
 Summary: Describes the beginning of the Spanish mission system in California, its expansion, and the effects of the missions on the native peoples of that area.
 ISBN 0-7565-0208-X (hardcover)
 1. California—History—To 1846—Juvenile literature. 2. Missions, Spanish—California—History—Juvenile literature. 3. Serra, Junípero, 1713–1784—Juvenile literature. 4. Franciscans—Missions—California—History—Juvenile literature. 5. Indians of North America—Missions—California—Juvenile literature. [1. Missions—California—History. 2. California—History—To 1846. 3. Serra, Junípero, 1713–1784. 4. Indians of North America—Missions—California.] I. Title. II. Series: We the people (Compass Point Books)
 F864 .H45 2002
 979.4'02—dc21   2001004743

TABLE OF CONTENTS

FROM WILDERNESS TO WONDERLAND

Only 250 years ago, the region that is now California was a vast wilderness along the Pacific Ocean. Its native people lived among mountains, seashores, deserts, and plains. They lived just as their ancestors had done for thousands of years. They fished along the coast and hunted animals in the forests and mountains. They gathered herbs, roots, nuts, and berries. Where oak trees grew, they ground the acorns into meal. Those who lived in pine tree country ate the piñon nuts.

Today, California is the third-largest state in the United States after Alaska and Texas. It is a world-famous wonderland—home to Hollywood, Disneyland, and the Los Angeles Lakers. California also has the largest population of all the states. About one out of every eight Americans lives there. It is hard to imagine California without its highways, skyscrapers, and celebrities.

These Native Americans lived in California's Sierra Nevada Mountains.

Los Angeles is the biggest city in California today.

How did that vast, quiet wilderness become the California we know today? The change began with the building of the California missions. These religious communities were the region's first European settlements. Twenty-one missions were built on the Pacific Coast, from San Diego to Sonoma—a distance of about 600 miles (965 kilometers).

The San Diego Mission was founded in 1769.

The map legend reads:

✝ Mission
● Pueblo
••••• El Camino Real
Map shows present-day boundaries.

California

Nevada

Utah

Sacramento

San Francisco Solano
San Rafael Arcángel
San Francisco de Asís
Santa Clara de Asís
San José
San José de Guadalupe
Santa Cruz
Santa Cruz
San Juan Bautista
San Carlos Borromeo
Nuestra Señora de la Soledad
San Antonio de Padua
San Miguel Arcángel
San Luis Obispo de Tolusa
La Purísima Concepción
Santa Inés
Santa Bárbara
San Fernando Rey de España
San Gabriel Arcángel
San Buenaventura
Los Angeles
San Juan Capistrano
San Luis Rey de Francia
San Diego de Alcalá

Pacific Ocean

Arizona

Colorado

N

0   40   80 miles
0   40   80 kilometers

MEXICO

The locations of the California missions

This car speeds up Highway 101 along the Pacific Ocean in northern California.

Each mission was about a day's journey by horseback from the next. The dusty trail that joined them was called *El Camino Real*, meaning "the Royal Highway." Today, California's Highway 101 covers almost the same route as El Camino Real.

Lower and Upper California

Spanish explorers arrived in present-day Mexico in the early sixteenth century. They also claimed a long **peninsula** in the northwest corner of Mexico. The peninsula was called *Baja California*, meaning "Lower California." The large region north of the peninsula was called *Alta California*, or "Upper California." It stretched from Mexico up through present-day California and beyond. Spain believed that Alta California extended through

Alta California extended north into the present-day state of California.

10

British traders hunted sea otters in California for their fur.

Canada to the coast of Alaska.

At first, Spain did not settle the northern territory of Upper California. King Carlos was too busy with the colonies in Mexico, known as New Spain. In time, however, Russian fur traders began traveling into Alta California. British traders in Canada were moving closer, too. These traders were hunting for sea otters, whose silky skins brought high prices in Europe.

King Carlos III wanted Spain to settle all of California.

By 1768, King Carlos knew he had to act. If Spain didn't settle the territory soon, some other country would. He sent a message to José Gálvez, his representative in New Spain. The king told Gálvez to settle Alta California right away. Spain had already built missions in Baja California. Gálvez decided that building missions was the perfect way to settle Upper California, too.

FATHER JUNÍPERO SERRA

Roman Catholic priests helped Spain build the California missions between 1769 and 1823. Their leader was a short, humble man named Father Junípero Serra.

Father Serra grew up on the Spanish island of Majorca. In 1738, he became a Roman Catholic priest in the Franciscans, a Roman Catholic religious order. The Franciscan Order is a religious society started by Saint Francis of Assisi in the early thirteenth century. Franciscan priests are called friars. They promise to live a

Father Serra helped build the California missions.

life of poverty, good works, and prayer.

Father Serra was a university teacher in Spain. He was also a powerful preacher. What he wanted most, however, was to be a **missionary**. Finally, in 1750, he was sent to New Spain, which is now the country of Mexico.

For many years, Father Serra worked among the Indians in New Spain. He wanted to help the native people and teach them his religious beliefs. Father Serra worked hard—in spite of his poor health and a lame leg. When King Carlos ordered

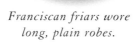

Franciscan friars wore long, plain robes.

14

José Gálvez decided that Spain should build missions throughout California.

José Gálvez to settle Alta California, Gálvez put Father Serra in charge. It would be difficult to set up missions in that rough territory. Gálvez knew the hardworking and well-loved Father Serra could do the job.

THE SACRED EXPEDITION

The journey to build the missions was called the Sacred **Expedition**. The Spanish governor—Gaspar de Portolá—was commander in chief of the project. Portolá gathered hundreds of people to help—soldiers, Franciscan friars, Mexican settlers, mule drivers, and American Indians. In 1769, Father Serra, Portolá, and the others set out from Baja California.

Some people traveled by land and some by sea. About half of the 300 sea travelers died on the trip. Father Serra and Portolá traveled with one of the two land groups. Many people in their group became sick and died along the way. Cutting the trail as they traveled, they headed north toward what is now San Diego.

The journey to Upper California was very difficult. Many people and animals died along the way.

THE FIRST MISSIONS

When Father Serra's group arrived in San Diego in July 1769, the priest planted a large wooden cross in the ground. He gathered the weary travelers around the cross and said a **Mass,** giving thanks for their safe arrival and asking for blessings on the new mission. Later, each time he built a new mission, Father Serra always began with this same ceremony.

California's first mission was called San Diego de Alcalá. It was named after a Spanish saint who was a Franciscan friar in the fifteenth century. In 1602, the Spanish explorer Sebastián Vizcaíno had named the nearby bay after this saint, too. The mission and the fort built by Father Serra and Portolá were the first Spanish settlements in what is now the state of California.

Father Serra and some others stayed on in San Diego to start the mission. Portolá and his men continued north, cutting a trail up the California coast that was later known

Father Serra placed a wooden cross in the ground. Then he gave thanks for his group's safe arrival in Upper California.

19

In 1776, Father Serra started the San Juan Capistrano Mission.

as El Camino Real. For the next fifty-four years, Franciscan friars followed that trail as they established missions in Alta California.

Father Serra started the first eight missions. After San Diego, they were San Carlos Borromeo in 1770; San Antonio de Padua and San Gabriel Arcángel in 1771; San Luis Obispo de Tolusa in 1772; San Francisco de Asís and San Juan Capistrano in 1776; Santa Clara de Asís in 1777; and San Buenaventura in 1782. Father Serra lived at Mission San Carlos Borromeo, near Monterey Bay. He died there in 1784, and friars carried on his work.

Today, this sign marks the location of El Camino Real.

THE MISSION COMPOUND

At first, the missions were just crude shelters. Later, the friars built sturdy, thick-walled buildings. They built them with adobe bricks. Adobe is a strong material made of clay and straw. The roofs of the missions were made of red-clay tiles in the Spanish style.

Some missions were built using adobe bricks.

As the missions grew, more buildings were added. Each group of buildings was called a compound. A mission compound was like a small town. It also had thousands of acres of farming and grazing land. At the center of the

compound was the
church, which had a tall
bell tower. Weddings
were held in the mission
church. Babies were
baptized there, too.

This baptismal font was used in
ceremonies at the Carmel Mission.

In front of the
church was a wide court-
yard called a plaza.
Across the plaza, facing
the church, was the entry
gate. The plaza was a kind
of village square. It had a fountain in the center and shad-
ed walkways along the sides. Workshops, storehouses, and
the friars' rooms stood around the patio, along with rooms
for the Indians and a mission school for their children.

Usually, a few Mexican soldiers lived inside the mission compounds. Some missions also had a nearby *presidio*
(military fort). The presidios protected the missions from

The Santa Bárbara Mission had a garden with a large fountain and many trees.

attacks by Indians, foreign trappers, and settlers from
the East.

As the missions grew, Indians settled in villages
around them. Many Mexicans settled around the missions,
too. Others traveled north to Alta California to make a
new life. Their communities were called pueblos. The first
pueblos were San Jose, Los Angeles, and Santa Cruz.
Today, Los Angeles is the largest city, by area, in the
United States.

This presidio guarded the missions near San Francisco.

DAILY LIFE AT THE MISSION

The friars taught the Indians about the Christian faith. Indians who **converted** came to live in the mission. There, they learned to raise crops and farm the fields. Some learned to herd cattle across the rolling ranges. Some learned trades and became blacksmiths and brick makers.

On some missions, Indians learned to make baskets and ropes.

Early in the morning, everyone living in the mission would be called to Mass.

Others learned to tan animal hides or make wine. Women spun cotton and wool to weave cloth. Some made pottery. Others made soap and candles from animal fat.

A typical day in the mission began early in the morning. In the bell tower, a friar pulled the heavy ropes that rang the bells. The ringing bells called everyone to the church for morning Mass. After Mass, everyone ate breakfast together. Then the adults began their work for the day. The children took their places in the classrooms. Some children studied the Spanish language and the Catholic religion. Older children learned a trade.

In the evening, everyone enjoyed music and dancing. Each mission had a band, with flutes, drums, and other musical instruments. Some churches had beautiful organs and choirs—and sometimes orchestras—for their religious services. When the nearby pueblos had *fiestas* (festivals), they invited Indian musicians to come and play.

SUCCESS AND FAILURE

The missions continued to grow. Hundreds, sometimes thousands, of people lived in each compound. The missionaries taught the Indians to grow vegetables and fruits. The fields were full of wheat, corn, and other crops. By the 1820s, the California missions had tens of thousands of cattle and sheep. Spanish ships sailed into ports along the California coast to deliver supplies. They left with a cargo of hides, animal fat, and wine from the missions.

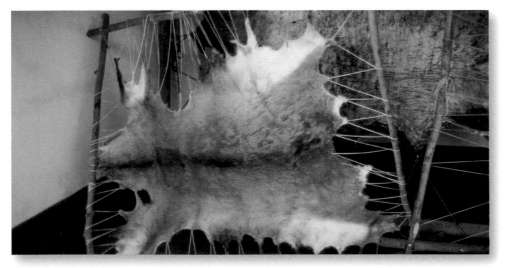

Animal hides were part of the cargo carried by Spanish ships.

The missions were not a complete success, however. At the end of the first year, the friars at the San Diego de Alcalá mission had not converted any of the Indians to the Christian faith. After five years, they had converted fewer than 100 Indians.

Before the missions arrived, California was home to more than 300,000 native people. Each tribe was made up of groups of relatives who lived together in villages. The Indians who moved to the missions were called Mission Indians. They were separated from their relatives and villages. They spoke a new language and followed a new religion. They had to wear different clothing and eat new foods—foods that sometimes made them sick. Hundreds of Indians also died from strange new illnesses brought to California by the Spaniards. Some Indians adjusted to their new lives—but many did not. They were confused and homesick and ran back to their villages.

There were other problems, too. The missionaries tried to convert the Indians by preaching and doing acts of kindness. But when the priests did not succeed, the soldiers took over. The soldiers often used force to move Indians into the compounds. Father Serra hated this situation and tried to stop the soldiers—but often he could not. Some of the soldiers beat the Indians. The friars themselves often forced order by beating the Indians.

Some Mission Indians lived in brush huts.

Spanish settlers were also acting badly. They were grazing their cattle on native lands, stealing Indian property, and attacking Indian women. Finally, the Indians became angry. On November 3, 1775, Indians from more than a dozen villages attacked the San Diego mission. Some of the attackers were Indians who had converted to the new religion.

The Franciscan friars did not blame the Indians for the attacks. The priests continued teaching and working in the missions. By 1833, about 88,000 Indians had been baptized.

THE END OF THE MISSION ERA

While the missions were expanding, the colonists of New Spain were growing restless. They no longer wanted to be ruled by a king in faraway Spain. They had seen the American colonies win their independence from Britain. Now they wanted to be independent, too. The Mexican Revolution began in 1810.

This mural by Juan O'Gorman depicts the Hidalgo Rebellion during the Mexican Revolution.

In 1821, Mexico won its independence from Spain. The next year, Mexico claimed Alta California as its province. The missions, with their churches and friars, had been Spain's project. The Mexicans had managed to get rid of Spain. Now they wanted to get rid of the missions, too. San Francisco Solano, which opened in 1823, was the last of the California missions.

In 1834, the government of Mexico began to take over the missions. They sent the friars away and freed the Indians. By law, the Indians were supposed to get half of the mission lands and cattle. Instead, most of the Indians were tricked out of their property or lost it in unfair deals.

Mexican governors sold or gave away hundreds of thousands of acres of mission land. In 1845, Governor Pío Pico sold fifteen of the twenty-one missions to private landowners. The new owners were called *rancheros* (ranchers). They hired Indians to work on their large ranches and farms.

Mexican governor Pío Pico sold some of the missions to ranchers.

Many of the new settlers were white people of
Spanish ancestry. Some came from Mexico. Others had
been soldiers in the presidios. Some of the settlers were
mestizos—people of mixed Spanish and Indian ancestry.

Americans wanted some of the free land, too.
Trappers and settlers traveled into the region along the

35

*The Battle of Palo Alto was the first battle of the Mexican War.
It took place near Brownsville, Texas, in 1846.*

California trail. In 1846, the United States government
seized California. That year, Texas went to war with
Mexico over land rights. Mexico lost the war—and
lost California.

     Then, in 1848, gold was discovered in California.
The population boomed as many people arrived to seek
their fortunes.

THE MISSIONS TODAY

In 1850, California became the thirty-first state in the United States. Soon, more Americans moved there and the mission lands were divided up even further. The buildings in the mission compounds became homes, offices, barns, and storehouses. Many buildings were torn down or just left to crumble. Finally, in 1865, President Abraham Lincoln ordered all the mission churches and grounds to be returned to the Roman Catholic Church.

President Abraham Lincoln returned the missions to the Roman Catholic Church.

Today, many of the old mission buildings have been rebuilt or restored. Some are national historic landmarks and belong to state or national parks. These old mission

The San Juan Capistrano Mission is known for its swallows and swallows' nests.

sites welcome thousands of visitors each year. They provide a glimpse of what life was like back then. The mission at Santa Bárbara is often called the Queen of the Missions. There is still a Franciscan school and church there. La Purísima Concepción is the largest mission still standing. It is also a state historic park. Mission San Francisco's Presidio is now a scenic forest overlooking San Francisco Bay. Old military buildings still stand along its winding trails.

The mission at San Juan Capistrano is probably the most famous California mission. It is best known for its swallows. Thousands of these graceful birds sweep in to nest there each spring. The friars noticed that the swallows arrived on March 19—St. Joseph's Day—and flew away on October 23—the anniversary of St. John of Capistrano's death. As the legend of the swallows spread, people came from miles around to watch them return every year. Visitors from around the world still travel to San Juan Capistrano to see the birds.

On the statue pedestal:

·PADRE·
·JVNIPERO·
·SERRA·
·FOVNDER·
·OF·THE·
·CALIFORNIA·
·MISSIONS·
·1713–1784·

A statue of Father Serra stands in San Francisco's Golden Gate Park.

Father Junípero Serra has also not been forgotten. The Catholic Church declared him "venerable" in 1985 and "blessed" in 1988. These are the first steps taken to make a person a saint. A large bronze statue of Father Serra stands in San Francisco's Golden Gate Park. In 1884, the legislature of California declared August 29—the 100th anniversary of his death—a legal holiday.

Glossary

baptized—admitted into the Christian faith with a spiritual ceremony

converted—changed from one faith to another

expedition—a long journey made for a special reason

Mass—a Roman Catholic religious service

missionary—a person sent by a religious group to spread their faith

peninsula—a strip of land that is almost completely surrounded by water and attached to a larger piece of land

Did You Know?

- Mission San Juan Bautista in Monterey County was featured in the Alfred Hitchcock movie *Vertigo*.

- Gold was discovered at the Mission San Fernando Rey de España in Los Angeles County in 1842.

- From 1769 to 1845, 146 Franciscan friars worked in the California missions.

- In 1932, Father Serra's birthplace in Majorca, Spain, became the property of the City of San Francisco, California.

IMPORTANT DATES

Timeline

1768	King Carlos of Spain asks José Gálvez to settle California.
1769	Father Junípero Serra opens San Diego de Alcalá, the first mission in what is now the state of California.
1775	Indians attack the San Diego mission.
1784	Father Serra dies at San Carlos Borromeo.
1821	Mexico wins independence from Spain.
1822	Mexico claims California.
1823	The twenty-first—and last—mission is founded at Sonoma.
1834–1835	Mexico takes over the missions.
1850	California becomes the thirty-first U.S. state.
1865	President Lincoln returns the mission lands to the Roman Catholic Church.

IMPORTANT PEOPLE

CARLOS (CHARLES) III
(1716–1788), *king of Spain, who ordered the settlement of Alta California*

JOSÉ GÁLVEZ
(1720–1787), *representative of King Carlos, in charge of settling Alta California*

PÍO PICO
(1801–1894), *second Mexican governor of California*

GASPAR DE PORTOLÁ
(c. 1723–c. 1784), *Spanish governor of Baja California and commander in chief of the Sacred Expedition*

FATHER JUNÍPERO SERRA
(1713–1784), *Franciscan missionary who founded the first California mission*

WANT TO KNOW MORE?

At the Library

Krall, Dorothy, editor. *California Missions: A Pictorial History*. Menlo Park, Calif.: Lane Publishing, 1979.

Nelson, Libby and Kari A. Cornell. *Projects & Layouts: California Missions*. Minneapolis: Lerner Publications, 1997.

Van Steenwyk, Elizabeth. *The California Missions*. New York: Franklin Watts, 1995.

On the Web

California Missions

http://www.bgmm.com/missions/

For more historical information about each mission

California Missions Studies Association

http://www.ca-missions.org

For information about the history and people of the California missions, presidios, and pueblos, and a link to the addresses of all the missions

California Museum of Photography: California Missions

http://www.cmp.ucr.edu/exhibitions/missions/

For great pictures from each of the twenty-one California missions

Through the Mail

San Diego de Alcalá and Mission Museum

10818 San Diego Mission Road

San Diego, CA 92108

619/281-8449

For more information about the first mission

On the Road

La Purísima Mission State Historic Park

2295 Purísima Road

RFD Box 102, La Purísima

Lompoc, CA 93436

805/733-1303

For living-history programs on mission life and Native American life during the Spanish and Mexican periods in California

Sonoma State Historic Park

114 East Spain Street

Sonoma, CA 95476

707/938-1519

To tour the last mission built in California

INDEX

About the Author

Ann Heinrichs grew up in Fort Smith, Arkansas. She began playing the piano at age three and thought she would grow up to be a pianist. Instead, she became a writer. Now she has written more than fifty books for children and young adults. Several of her books have won national awards. Ms. Heinrichs now lives in Chicago, Illinois. She enjoys martial arts and traveling to faraway countries.